FIGHT FOR SURVIVAL

The Story of the Holocaust

BY JESSICA FREEBURG

Consultant:
Tim Solie
Adjunct Professor of History
Minnesota State University, Mankato

CAPSTONE PRESS
a capstone imprint

Tangled History is published by Capstone Press,
1710 Roe Crest Drive, North Mankato, Minnesota 56003
www.mycapstone.com

Library of Congress Cataloging-in-Publication Data
Names: Freeburg, Jessica, author.
Title: Fight for survival : the story of the Holocaust / by Jessica Freeburg.
Description: North Mankato, MN : Capstone Press, [2017]
Series: Tangled history | Includes bibliographical references and index. |
Audience: Age 8–14, grade 4 to 6.
Identifiers: LCCN 2016009134|
ISBN 9781491484548 (library binding) |
ISBN 9781491484586 (paperback) |
ISBN 9781491484623 (ebook pdf)
Subjects: LCSH: Holocaust, Jewish (1939-1945)—Juvenile literature.
Classification: LCC D804.34 .F74 2017 | DDC 940.53/180922—dc23
LC record available at http://lccn.loc.gov/2016009134

Editorial Credits
Adrian Vigliano, editor; Heidi Thompson, designer; Svetlana Zhurkin, media
researcher; Tori Abraham, production specialist

Photo Credits
Alamy: Agencja Fotograficzna Caro, 75, Image Bank, 15, Interfoto, 76, Sueddeutsche
Zeitung Photo, 6, 18, 42; DVIC: NARA, 4; Getty Images: Galerie Bilderwelt, 105, Hulton
Archive, 90, Popperfoto, 35, The LIFE Picture Collection/William Vandivert, 30, UIG/
Sovfoto, 89; Library of Congress, 71; Newscom: akg-images, 51, 52, dpa/picture-
alliance/DENA, 12, World History Archive, 58, ZUMA Press/Jürgen Stroop, cover

TABLE OF CONTENTS

FOREWORD

In 1919, on the heels of the loss to the Allied Powers in World War I, Germany begrudgingly signed a treaty accepting responsibility for the conflict. The nation had lost many territories and was also ordered to pay for damages sustained during the war. As a result, many Germans despaired as the economy crumbled around them. When war hero Adolf Hitler became the leader of the National Socialist German Workers' (Nazi) Party, the struggling middle class was desperate for hope.

Using propaganda, Hitler placed the blame for Germany's problems on anyone who was not a member of the Aryan race, which consisted of white, non-Jewish Germans. The Nazis spread their message of hate through newspaper cartoons that belittled Jewish men, women, and children. By 1928, more than 100,000 Germans had pledged their allegiance to the Nazi Party.

Hitler officially rose to power when he was named the chancellor of Germany on January 30, 1933. As his power grew and his control of the government became more complete, life for Jews in Germany became increasingly difficult. In an effort to remove Jews from positions of influence, those who worked as civil servants or in newspaper publishing were fired. The Nazis also eliminated many Jewish-owned businesses. Jewish doctors were only permitted to provide services to other Jews.

By 1935, all Jews were no longer considered citizens. They, along with other minorities, became targets of legal segregation and public humiliation. While many Jews emigrated to less hostile areas, many others remained in Germany. But the situation would only get worse for the Jews. Much worse.

1

A CRY FOR JUSTICE

Herschel Grynszpan (center)

Herschel Grynszpan

Seventeen-year-old Herschel Grynszpan held the postcard from his sister, Berta, in his trembling hand. He had read her message so many times since receiving the postcard four days earlier that he didn't need to look at it to know what it said. The words felt as if they'd been chiseled into his brain.

Herschel had lived in France since 1936. With his parents' blessing, he had made the move as growing discrimination against Jews made it clear that he had no future in Germany. Now the Nazis had arrested his family. He'd heard rumors that thousands of others had been arrested, as well. Their crime was nothing more than being Jewish. For this, they were deprived of their possessions, packed into railroad cars until they had no room to sit down, and sent to Lodz, Poland. They had been treated more like a herd of animals than human beings. He read Berta's words once more.

"No one told us what was up, but we realized this was going to be the end ... We haven't a penny. Could you send us something?"

Herschel set the card aside, then picked up a fresh postcard and began to write a response. A short time later, he made his way through Paris, finally arriving at the locked gates of the German Embassy. There he spotted a well-dressed man arriving at the building.

"I must speak to a member of the diplomatic staff," Herschel said, trying to conceal the tremor in his voice.

"You need to speak to our doorman, Mathes, to be let in," the man replied before walking casually inside.

Herschel took a deep breath, then calmly turned to the doorman and said, "I have some important documents for the ambassador."

Once inside, Herschel could feel his heart pounding in his chest. It had been easy enough getting into the building, but the worst part was yet to come.

He had never pointed a gun at another human being and then pulled the trigger before. Now he wondered if he could go through with it. But then he thought again of his family cruelly packed inside a train car and felt the anger rising inside him. They were good people, ripped away from the life they had worked so hard to create. He thought of them thrown into a world where even hope had been taken from them.

He could not forgive these arrests, this horrible treatment of his family and other Jews by the Germans. He knew it was up to him to stand up and do something to avenge the Jewish people. Herschel pulled a postcard from his pocket and looked again at the words he had written in response to Berta's message: "May God forgive me, I must protest so that the whole world hears my protest, and that I will do."

Looking up he realized he was approaching someone. It was a secretary, working at a desk situated outside of a door.

"May I help you?" asked the secretary.

"I have important documents I must deliver to a member of the diplomatic staff," Herschel said.

The secretary picked up his desk phone. After a brief conversation, he pointed toward the office door. "Go ahead."

Herschel drew a shaky breath before knocking.

"Come in," said a voice from inside the office.

Herschel entered the room. The door shut behind him. Everything seemed silent, except for the sound of the secretary typing in the corridor. Then Herschel aimed his gun at the man behind the desk and shattered the silence with gunshots.

Joseph Goebbels

Munich, Germany,
November 9, 1938, evening

German Minister of Propaganda Joseph Goebbels was attending a reception with Adolf Hitler and other members of the Nazi Party. Earlier, he had received word of diplomat Ernst vom Rath's death. Apparently, a man named Herschel Grynszpan had entered the German Embassy in Paris and shot vom Rath. Grynszpan had been arrested and was in the custody of the French officials.

Now Joseph walked toward the podium. The crowd had gathered to hear Hitler, but they were unaware that Joseph would speak instead of Hitler. Joseph had given many speeches in the five years he had served as the propaganda minister for the Nazi Party. He had become comfortable with such public events long ago, but tonight he could hardly contain his emotion as he looked over his audience.

"I have news for you here tonight," he began, "to demonstrate what happens to a good German when he drops his guard for one moment. Ernst vom Rath was a good German, working for the good of our people in our embassy in Paris. Shall I tell you what happened to him?" The crowd hung on his words, silently waiting for what he would say next.

"He was shot down!" Joseph continued, slamming his fist against the podium. A wave of shocked voices rippled through the audience. "In the course of his duty, he went, unarmed and unsuspecting, to speak to a visitor at the embassy, and had two bullets pumped into him. He is now dead … Do I need to tell you the race of the dirty swine who perpetrated this foul deed? A Jew!"

Joseph Goebbels

Shock turned to anger as the voices of the crowd began to rise in outrage. Joseph stepped back from the podium and gazed over the crowd. He knew his words had incited outrage in the crowd. The fury he had poured into his words had sparked a fire within all who heard them, just as he'd hoped.

After the reception, Hitler sent orders to the

German police to protect non-Jewish businesses and residences, but to allow the destruction of Jewish property. The police were also directed to immediately begin arresting healthy Jewish men and teens and to prepare them for transfer to prison camps.

Returning to his hotel later that evening, Joseph looked out the window of his car and saw that the destruction had already begun. He rolled down his window to the sound of breaking glass and a glowing vision of fire from a burning synagogue.

Fred Spiegel

Dinslaken, Germany,
November 10, 1938, morning

Six-year-old Fred Spiegel woke up early, excited to have breakfast with Mr. and Mrs. Brockhausen. The couple rented an apartment from Fred's family on the third floor of their home. He spent many a happy morning with the kind, elderly couple.

Looking out the window, Fred saw smoke rising against the sky and men running past with pick axes.

"Mother, what is going on outside?" he asked.

His mother glanced out the window. "I'm not sure," she replied.

Fred made his way up to the Brockhausen's apartment for breakfast. Maybe they could tell him what was going on. He found Mrs. Brockhausen busy preparing food.

"Did you see the smoke outside? Where do you think it's coming from?" Fred asked.

"The synagogue is on fire," Mr. Brockhausen replied. "But the fire engines are already there." He patted Fred on the back. "Not to worry. The fire will surely be put out soon."

The clinks and clangs of breakfast being put together were disrupted by a horrific bang that came from the direction of Fred's apartment. The sound of breaking glass was drowned out by the piercing screams of Fred's mother and his sister, Edith.

Fred's father had passed away years before, and although his grandfather lived with them, he still felt in many ways like he was the man of the house. He wanted to protect his mother and sister from whatever awful thing was happening in their apartment, but Mr. Brockhausen held him back.

His body shook with fear as he listened to things being smashed in his apartment below and glass shattering on the ground outside as things were thrown out the window.

When the destruction stopped, Fred hurried downstairs and found his mother and sister on the balcony. They were looking down at the broken crystal and smashed furniture that had been part of their peaceful home only moments before. Now everything was upturned and in disarray.

"Your grandfather has been arrested," Fred's mother said, her voice tight with terror, her face showing a fear he'd never seen before.

Over 1,000 synagogues and 7,500 Jewish businesses were destroyed on November 9 and 10, 1938. This event became known as Kristallnacht.

In the 16 years of his life, Arnold Blum had never before been so angry. He stood in the flicker of the blazing synagogue, not daring to protest what he witnessed. He knew if he spoke against the vandals, his life would be in grave danger.

Members of the fire brigade stood nearby protecting some of the surrounding buildings—those not owned by Jews— as the flames licked toward them. They worked to keep the fire from spreading, but did nothing to save the holy place. Now the walls crumbled, leaving an empty shell of what once was.

Arnold clenched his fists, his eyes filled with tears as he silently prayed, "Rise up, Lord, and scatter your enemies." But all that rose up were curls of smoke.

Two Gestapo men burst into
the ransacked apartment. "You will
come with us," one of them ordered
without explanation.

Fred's mother took a deep breath
and tried to put on a brave face as she
and her children followed the man. The
other Gestapo man walked behind them,
hurrying them along.

Soon, they were walking in the streets
with other Jewish families. Germans lined
their path, spitting and throwing rocks.
Their walk ended at the Jewish school,
where they were forced to stay.

Fred couldn't understand what they
had done to deserve to be treated in such
a way. He had never been so scared.

THE CRIME OF BEING JEWISH

2

The Nazis forced Jewish people to identify themselves with items such as the Star of David.

Arnold Blum

Stuttgart, Germany,
November 11, 1938, 6:00 a.m.

When the doorbell rang, Arnold was not surprised. He had seen the Gestapo men coming when he peered through his window, their flashlights cutting through the darkness of the early morning. He was terrified, however, the fear twisting his stomach as he opened the door.

"Is there an Arnold Blum living here?" one of the men asked curtly.

"You are speaking to him," Arnold replied, trying to conceal his fear.

"How old are you?"

"Sixteen."

"You are under arrest."

"But why?" Arnold asked in shock. He had broken no laws, but he knew that his crime might simply be that he was Jewish.

"You are placed under protective custody," the man replied with no explanation.

Soon Arnold and his uncle, Bruno Stern, were preparing to leave with the Gestapo. Uncle Bruno took his time with a cup of coffee and breakfast. Arnold couldn't bring himself to eat anything. His stomach was in knots with anxiety.

"How long will they be gone?" Arnold's mother asked as she prepared two slices of bread for Arnold to take in his pocket.

"Not long," one of the Gestapo men replied.

Arnold's mother and grandmother wept as he kissed them before being escorted away with his uncle. They walked in silence through the cold, damp air. The sun was just beginning to rise. What should have been a beautiful sight was clouded by dread and fear.

After spending part of the day in a local police station cell, Arnold and his uncle were transported to the large central police station. They were herded into a cell crowded with other Jewish detainees, where they were pressed body to body. They stood like this for hours. A suffocating stench came from the corner of the cell where a pail was the only toilet.

Eventually they were led outside, where buses waited for them. Arnold realized that he would not be returning home soon, as the Gestapo man had told his mother.

"You will leave tonight for Dachau," a soldier said.

Arnold climbed aboard the bus, his mind hazy with uncertainty. He was leaving behind his home and traveling to a labor camp. He had no choice. The thought frightened him because he knew it meant he was losing his freedom. He looked around at the faces of the men who were being deported with him. Many of them he had known most of his life. He wondered when he would see his family again.

Hours later, the bus door finally opened with a groan. The men on the bus wished they could groan, too, as they stood stooped in the aisle, their bodies aching from the long trip. But they dared not make a sound.

"Get off the bus! Move it!" an SS soldier ordered.

The men hurried, some stumbling on legs still terribly numb from the cramped bus, others helping them along.

"Line up!" another soldier shouted.

Arnold moved quickly into formation with other men. Buses unloaded around him. More dazed men spilled out and lined up as SS men barked orders at them.

Arnold watched, shocked, as an SS man dragged an unconscious man by the feet down the steps of the bus. The man's head bounced down each step like a child's ball. The pain seemed to revive him, and as he was flung into the dirt his leg accidentally hit the SS soldier. In a rage, the SS man stomped and kicked the victim mercilessly.

Arnold could hardly believe what he was seeing. He had never witnessed one human exact such brutality against another.

He couldn't imagine doing such a thing to another person.

The men were counted and ordered to march. Thousands of them, some already bruised from abuse, entered the camp. The men were marched to a large, open field where they were ordered to stand at attention. And there they stood for many hours.

Arnold watched as the sun sank beyond the horizon. He had seen the same sun rise that morning as he was forced to walk toward the living nightmare in which he now stood. His legs cramped from standing so long and he was weak from hunger. The only food he'd eaten all day were the two slices of bread his mother had slipped into his pocket.

Arnold guessed it was 9:00 p.m. when the men were finally marched to a barracks.

"Remove your shoes. Place them neatly in a line so you can find them in the morning." The SS man looked at the imprisoned men with disgust as they did what he had ordered.

Inside the barracks, they were met by the kapo assigned to them. He was a prisoner as well, and they learned he had been assigned to maintain order and control of his fellow inmates. His head was shaved and he wore a uniform marked with a green triangle.

"I am imprisoned here for political offenses. I was a Communist tailor from Bad Cannstatt, near Stuttgart," he said. "Please raise your hand if you are over the age of 90."

Two men raised their hands and gave their ages. One was 92 and the other was 96. Pointing at the older of the two, the kapo said, "You will have my bed. I will take the floor." He then began to cut up a chunk of bread. "I know it is not much, but it is all I can offer you. Please take a little and pass it around so that every man has some to eat."

Arnold was moved by the kapo's kindness as he realized the man was sacrificing his own ration of food for them. In the washroom he cleaned himself with cold water and dried off with his handkerchief, then he joined the other prisoners back in the barracks.

He stood near one of the straw-covered platforms that would serve as a bed. "Please, take this one," he said to an elderly man as he motioned toward the bunk. The other young men did the same. Soon everyone had settled into a place to try to sleep, although they had no blankets.

Arnold looked for a place to squeeze in on the floor with the other young men. They were packed so tightly into the room that there was no place left for him. He finally settled himself across other people's legs.

"I'm sorry," he said in a hushed voice.

"It's fine," one boy replied. "I am so tired, I could sleep with a boulder on me."

Arnold Blum

Dachau Concentration Camp, Germany,
November 12, 1938, 5:00 a.m.

Morning came quickly, and Arnold felt as if he had hardly slept at all. Other men moving about had stepped on him several times in the night. Seeing that washing himself would be impossible in the crowded rush of people in the washroom, he rinsed his mouth with water and returned to the barracks.

"You will need to get your shoes on and stand in formation," the kapo said. "An officer will take you to be processed."

When Arnold exited the barracks, he was shocked to see all the shoes they had lined neatly along the outer wall heaped into one immense pile. An SS man smirked at him. Arnold hurried to the mountain of shoes and began to search for a pair large enough to fit him. Soon the rest of the men from the barracks were digging through the pile.

"Hurry up!" the SS man yelled.

In his haste, Arnold took two shoes that were

too small, but he crammed his feet into them and fell into formation.

"March!"

The men marched, their mismatched shoes raising a small cloud of dust. They entered an administration building, where they had to wait to be photographed and fingerprinted.

Arnold followed those in front of him in line into the next room, where they were ordered to undress. He felt ashamed as he stood completely naked. He watched as other prisoners gathered the neatly folded piles of clothing and took them away.

Next he was directed to a wooden bench, where another prisoner shaved his hair with electric clippers. Still naked and in utter dismay at what was happening, Arnold was herded into a shower with other bewildered men. As the prisoners left the shower, SS soldiers laughed and mocked them while hosing them off with harsh blasts of water.

Wet and shivering, they were taken to another room, where an SS man gave them a physical exam. After the exam they were finally given clothing. Their prisoner garb was made of thin cotton, covered in black and white stripes, and marked with a yellow Star of David, the Jewish holy symbol.

Arnold was anxious to cover himself. He found that his pants were far too short, barely covering his knees. In addition the waist was so large that he struggled to pull the drawstring tight enough to keep the garment on. The sleeves on his prison shirt reached only slightly below his elbows. He looked around at his fellow inmates—each in similarly ill-fitting uniforms—and shook his head.

Arnold felt as if his sense of time was slipping, but it seemed like they had been processed for hours before they were finally marched to their permanent barracks.

At the barracks the group was given one spoon each, an aluminum pot for two of them to use instead of a plate or bowl while eating, and one toothbrush for four inmates to share. Arnold felt the pain of hunger grab at his abdomen, and he realized he had not eaten since the night before when the kind kapo had distributed small bits of bread.

After the inmates were assigned places to sleep, the kapo went over the camp rules.

"You no longer have a name. You will only be called by your prisoner number," the kapo began. "There is a grass strip running along the inside of the barbed wire fence. Do not step onto the strip, even if you are ordered to do so. You will be shot by one of the guards from the towers or on the ground."

Arnold looked around at the faces of the other inmates. Some seemed too exhausted and hungry for expression. They simply looked blank. Others bore bruised and swollen lumps that they must have been given during their transport to the camp. A few seemed to be holding back tears as the horror of their situation began to sink in.

"You will be marched to the drill field each morning, where you will be counted. You will not be fed until the SS has accepted the count. If anyone is unaccounted for, you will stay there until they are found. Anyone who dies must be carried to the field for the count."

Arnold wondered how many of these men now standing around him, weak and hungry but still very much alive, would suffer such a fate. He shuddered at the thought.

Arnold Blum

The prisoners had hurried in and out of the washroom and fell into formation outside the barracks. Still wearing the small shoes he had pulled from the pile days before, Arnold marched to the drill field with the other lines of inmates, his toes pinched and hurting, the skin on the heels of his feet blistered and beginning to bleed. His stomach ached with hunger. The cold air cut through the thin fabric of his uniform.

As he stood at attention, the sun began to rise. It created a brilliant red hue that brightened the darkness of the clear sky. Slowly, the brilliance of the sun rose above the horizon. He was taken with the beauty of it, and for the first time in the days following his arrest, he felt hope. This simple sunrise reminded him that there was something more powerful than Hitler and his legions of SS soldiers.

Silently, Arnold prayed, "Thank you, God, for giving us the sunrise as a sign of hope." He allowed the belief that he would survive to fill him with warmth and peace.

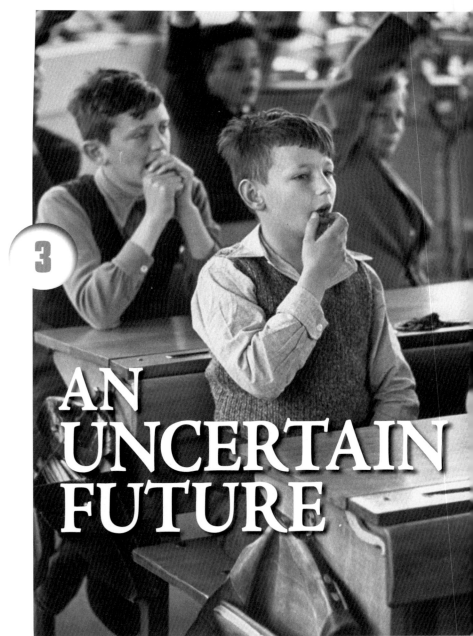

AN UNCERTAIN FUTURE

3

Dutch students attended classes and went on with their lives in 1939 as problems worsened in neighboring Germany.

Fred Spiegel

After the terror of the night the synagogue had burned, Fred's mother sent him and his older sister, Edith, to Holland to live with their Uncle Adolf and his family. Fred had been close with his extended family for as long as he could remember, so staying with them felt natural.

Now, Fred sat in the one-room schoolhouse among his new peers. He looked across the room to where Edith and their cousins, Margot and Alice, sat. Looking up, Alice gave him a small wave and a smile before returning her attention to her book.

"You're doing quite well," Mrs. Verbeist said, looking over Fred's shoulder at his arithmetic work.

"Thank you, Ma'am," he replied.

Mrs. Verbeist patted his shoulder before walking toward her desk. She rang a small bell to get the students' attention before announcing that school was dismissed. Fred joined his sister and cousins outside the schoolhouse for the walk home.

"When we get home, I will work with you and Edith on your Dutch," Alice said.

"Oh, thank you!" Edith replied. "I must admit, I feel a bit behind in my studies because I don't quite understand everything Mrs. Verbeist says in lectures."

"You will get it soon, and I will help you both as much as you need," Alice said, smiling, as they walked the road toward home.

"Me, too," Margot agreed.

Fred looked up at the clear sky. He missed his mother, but he was happy spending time with his cousins. He had settled into the new community and made friends quickly. Terror had shaken him in Germany, but here, he felt safe.

Maria Blitz

Krakow, Poland, Summer 1939

Maria Blitz looked down uncertainly at the diamond on her left hand. She was only 21 years old, and none of her friends had become engaged yet, but her father was sure Moses would be the perfect husband for her.

She had hoped to attend the local university, but there were so many incidences of Jews being beaten up by the Polish students that her father had forbidden it. She knew he was probably right to do so, but she still felt angry to see her choices limited simply because she was Jewish.

"Next," the banker behind the counter called out.

Maria stepped forward. "Good afternoon," she said politely as she handed over the deposit her father had asked her to make. Her father had been a good customer of the bank, and she recognized this gentleman as a banker who knew her father fairly well.

The man nodded, but did not return the greeting. "That's quite the ring you've got there," he said.

"Yes, I have just become engaged."

"That is why the rest of us have no money. You Jews took it all," the man grumbled as he processed her transaction.

Maria felt as if she had been slapped. No one had ever said such a thing to her before. She knew there was prejudice against the Jewish people in her community, but this was the first time it had affected her. Her family was wealthy, her father a prominent factory owner, and she, with her blonde hair and blue eyes, looked more like her Catholic friends than her Jewish ones.

Maria had heard others talk about the growing tension and anger directed at Jews, and she worried this might be just the beginning of the sort of animosity she would face.

Maria Blitz

Krakow, Poland, September 6, 1939

France officially declared war against Germany on September 3, 1939, just two days after the German invasion of Poland. Maria still wasn't sure how to feel about the news. Although the unknown of a war was frightening, she also hoped it might mean that if the Germans were defeated, the Jews would have more rights and face less persecution.

The bombs had fallen for five days, and Maria, along with her extended family, had hidden in her aunt's cellar. Then word spread that the Germans had entered Krakow and would kill any Jewish man or boy they found. Maria's brother and fiancé fled out of fear for their lives.

Now, just a few days later, Maria sat on another train with her sister-in-law and infant niece beside her. The door of the passenger car burst open and a German soldier stood in the doorway.

"Are there any Jews here?" he asked.

Blitz's sister-in-law began to raise her hand, but a Polish woman sitting with them nudged her. "Don't say anything," the woman whispered. She cleared her throat and said loudly, "No, there are no Jews."

The soldier left the car, closing the door behind him. Blitz let out a breath she was unaware she had been holding. For now, she had avoided trouble. She wasn't even sure what kind of trouble they would have faced if they had been identified, but she felt sure it was best to remain silent.

Krakow was a major city for culture and education before World War II.

Dawid Sierakowiak

The day began with a peaceful calm that was almost unsettling. In the days before, 15-year-old Dawid Sierakowiak had seen panic and fear in his family and friends as the Germans crossed the border of Poland. So many in Lodz had fled. Even the police were gone. But Dawid's family had chosen to stay. The sound of cannon blasts and the glow of red that rose up in the south confirmed that the fighting was close. But it was still difficult for Dawid to believe that the Germans would take Lodz. He prayed for a miracle.

When he heard the news that the Germans had arrived, Dawid was sketching a picture of his girlfriend in the park. "Lodz has been surrendered!" a boy called as he ran past Dawid.

"Without a fight?" Dawid called after him, but the boy ran on without responding.

Dawid gathered his notebook and pencils, and then hurried home. The streets were eerily quiet.

"Did you hear about the elders?" Dawid's friend Lolek asked.

"I heard yesterday that they had not returned home from their meeting," Dawid replied. Everyone in the community had been talking about the 22 Jews who were appointed by Nazis to the "Jewish Elders of Lodz" and their scheduled meeting with the German authorities.

"This morning, I heard that they had been arrested. But this afternoon, when I was in the city, I heard someone say they had been released," Lolek continued.

"I had hoped their meeting would make things easier for us," Dawid said. "But if they were arrested, it must not have gone well."

Things had become increasingly difficult and frightening in Lodz since the Germans took the city two months before. Jews were being rounded up for forced labor, Jewish shops were being looted, and the Nazis were going into Jewish homes at random, taking whatever they wanted.

Dawid had been forced to help the Germans steal from his own friends' families. They made him walk the streets for hours one evening. Along the way the soldiers made him carry the things they took. His load became so heavy his arms ached, and sweat dripped from his brow as he lugged the stolen possessions.

The price of food had skyrocketed, making it nearly impossible to afford anything. People waited in line for hours for a small loaf of bread, sometimes only to be sent away with nothing. Hunger and fear clouded the community. Everything felt uncertain.

Despite the horrible conditions, the boys felt determined to continue their studies. Classes were often canceled, but they attended school as often as possible.

"How did you do on the math test?" Lolek asked.

"I got an A," Dawid said with a smile.

"And you were so worried for nothing."

Maria Blitz

"Have you been waiting here long?" The deep voice of the German soldier startled Maria as she stood outside waiting for her friend.

"Yes, a while," she replied. She looked around anxiously, nervous to be seen speaking with a German. "Why do you ask?"

"Because I had a date with a girl, and she didn't show," the soldier replied.

"I haven't seen anybody."

"How come you speak such good German?" he asked.

"I learned it in school," she replied, still unsure if she should be seen speaking with the soldier.

A group of German soldiers in their green uniforms walked past. They gave the "Heil Hitler" salute to the man beside her as they walked past. He returned the salute.

"I left my mother at home in Germany. I am her only son, and I hated to leave her alone there. But then Hitler came in with his blockhead ideas, and here we are, stuck in a war."

Maria's heart beat fast as he spoke against Hitler. What if he was trying to bait her into saying something so he could find a reason to punish her?

"I don't know if you should be speaking to me like this," she said meekly. "Do you see that I am wearing a Jewish star?"

"It is that lousy Hitler who made those laws. You are people like any other people."

"I'm sorry," she said, still frightened by the turn in their conversation. "I really need to be going." She hurried away, too afraid to look back.

Dawid Sierakowiak

Lodz, Poland, February 8, 1940

When the official order came down that a ghetto would be established in Lodz, Dawid Sierakowiak wasn't sure what to think. He knew from his studies at school there were around 230,000 Jews living in Lodz, and he wondered how they would all fit into the space the Nazis were putting a fence around. When the fence was up, completely sealing them off from the rest of the city, fear settled on the community.

Dawid pulled the blanket tighter around him and closed his eyes against the hunger that made his stomach cramp with pain. He wasn't sure how long he had been in bed, trying to fall asleep, but it felt like a long time. He heard his mother and father speaking in hushed voices at the table.

"How can they expect us to pay rent or buy food when they won't allow us to earn money?" his father asked.

"They're giving us one loaf of bread for five days," his mother said, her voice thick with worry. "It's barely enough to stay alive. More people die each day from being sick and hungry."

"And others take their own lives in despair," his father whispered. "I never would have thought I'd understand such an action, but there is such hopelessness in this ghetto."

"We must remain hopeful," his mother replied.

"We will. There will be joy on the other side of this," his father said.

Closing his eyes tightly, Dawid prayed his father was right.

NO NEED TO BE AFRAID

Nazi troops invaded the Netherlands on May 10, 1940, catching the Dutch military unprepared.

The rays of the bright spring sun woke Fred Spiegel that morning. He stretched, rubbed his eyes, and smiled at the beginning of what promised to be a beautiful day. But what he saw below his window on the cobblestone streets startled him out of his happy awakening.

Soldiers with rifles, wearing battle gear, walked along the street beside tanks and trucks. The sky was speckled with airplanes bearing German markings.

Then Fred heard his Aunt Martha speaking German. An unfamiliar male voice responded. Quickly, Fred dressed and hurried downstairs.

To his shock, he saw a German soldier sitting at the kitchen table. Aunt Martha was preparing coffee. Fred's sister and their cousins sat in the living room, looking out the window at the commotion on the streets. Uncle Adolf was not in either room.

"Why do you speak such flawless German?" the soldier asked Aunt Martha.

"I am originally from Germany," she replied. "But it became too dangerous for me to live there because I am Jewish."

"Well, I have no problem with you being Jewish. There's no need to be afraid. We are not here to harm you," he assured her. Then he turned to Fred, who stood watching from the base of the steps. "And how old are you, young man?"

"Eight years old," Fred replied politely, trying to keep the fear out of his voice.

"I have a son your age," the man said. "I'm with a motorcycle unit parked across the street." He motioned toward the window. "Could you keep a lookout and let me know when my unit starts to move?"

"Yes," Fred replied, taking up a post near the window. He stood watch, hoping the unit would move soon. Although this particular German soldier had been civilized, Fred feared the Germans. He was frightened by the thought of what would become of the Jews now that Germany had invaded Holland.

At some point, around June 12, Herschel Grynszpan and the other inmates housed in the same prison were moved south by train. But during the trip, German planes attacked the train. When the dust of the attack settled, Herschel found himself free. He made his way through the countryside until he found himself in the French town of Toulouse. There, he turned himself in at the local jail.

"I do not think it is wise for you to stay here," Paul Ribeyre, the town's public prosecutor, said to Herschel. "The Germans are already closing in, and they are undoubtedly looking for you."

Herschel had spent the last two years in prison. He had grown from a quivering, frightened 17-year-old boy into an articulate young man. Although still small in stature, it seemed that those who met him respected him, perhaps in part because of what he had done to stand up to the Nazis. Regardless of how they felt about him, whether they thought what he had done was just or unjust, he had done something rare. He stood up against the Germans on behalf of his fellow Jews. Knowing that allowed him to carry himself with a certain amount of confidence he hadn't possessed before.

Herschel thanked Ribeyre for his advice and prepared to set out again. Although he was still tired from days of running after the convoy was attacked, he would continue trying to stay ahead of the Germans, who were getting closer and closer to his position.

Marta Munzer

Kamenets-Podolsk, Ukraine, August 1941

Marta Munzer stood above the pit, naked and shaking with fear, her hand clenched tightly around her mother's hand. She was not sure how many other women and children stood with her in the same shame and terror, but she guessed there were hundreds, maybe thousands lined up along the edge of the long trench.

It seemed like just yesterday she was riding her shiny red bicycle with her friend Eva Heyman along the streets of Nagyvarad. The two girls, not quite into their teens, parked their bikes in front of Eva's home and went inside. They were snacking on chocolate and strawberries with whipped cream, which was Marta's favorite thing to eat, when the Munzer family cook came to the door in a panic.

"Martika, come home. The police are there, and you have to go with Papa and Mama," the cook said, her voice tight with fear.

"It must be because I rode my bicycle so fast on Rimanoczi Street. Papa always tells me I will end up at the police for speeding," Marta reasoned.

But the police had not come on account of her speeding. They had come to take her family away. Marta was not even allowed to pack a suitcase. She was led away from her home with nothing but the clothes on her back.

"Where are they taking us?" she asked her mother.

"To Ukraine. There are homes for us there that were abandoned by the Jewish families who fled to the East."

They were herded into a train car like animals, one body pressed against another. The heat of the afternoon sun made the air thick and suffocating. They were given no food, and Marta's stomach began to ache with hunger before they reached their destination.

There was no home for the family in Ukraine. They had not been taken here to live, but to die.

Marta closed her eyes and prayed that the bullets would not hurt. Maybe God would spare her pain.

After all, she had been a good girl, surely he would grant her this one last request.

Eva Heyman
Nagyvarad, Hungary, September 1941

It had been a month since her friend, Marta Munzer, had left Eva Heyman's house. The memory of their final moments together had haunted Eva's thoughts every day since.

Eva's mother, Agi, had called Marta's grandmother repeatedly but had gotten no answer. Eva had tried to call Marta's home the next day, but she, too, got no answer. So her mother had gone into town and spoken to local journalists. She came home with the most awful news.

"Tens of thousands of people, including Marta's family, have been sent away by train, without luggage and without food," Agi said.

Now, weeks later, as Eva went into town with her mother, her heart still ached for sweet Marta. Beside the gate rested two red bicycles, exactly where the girls had left them that awful day. No one could bear to move them from that spot, and so there they stayed.

Herschel had made his way from one French town to another for several weeks, trying to stay one step ahead of the Nazis. His German pursuers always seemed to be close behind. When he arrived at the town of Bourges, exhausted and tired of running, he found the local prison and turned himself in.

On July 18, 1940, Herschel was sent back to Germany, and he became a prisoner of the Nazis. Eventually he became an inmate at Sachsenhausen Concentration Camp. There he waited to face trial for the murder of Ernst vom Rath. Herschel was assigned to a special bunker for inmates who received preferential treatment. He ate the same meals as the Nazis who guarded him. They wanted to keep him healthy for the spectacle of the trial they planned for him.

But then Hitler postponed the trial.

Herschel was told to prepare to be transferred.

"I wonder where they will take you," an inmate said as they sat together in the bunker.

"I cannot even guess," Herschel replied, his shoulders back and head high as he waited for the guards to come for him. "Don't think that I am afraid. When I reach the end I will spit three times on this sinister band of rogues."

Two SS men entered the bunker.

"Time to go," one of them said.

Herschel knew this could be the end, but he tried to show no fear. He walked boldly from the bunker to an uncertain fate.

Herschel Grynszpan

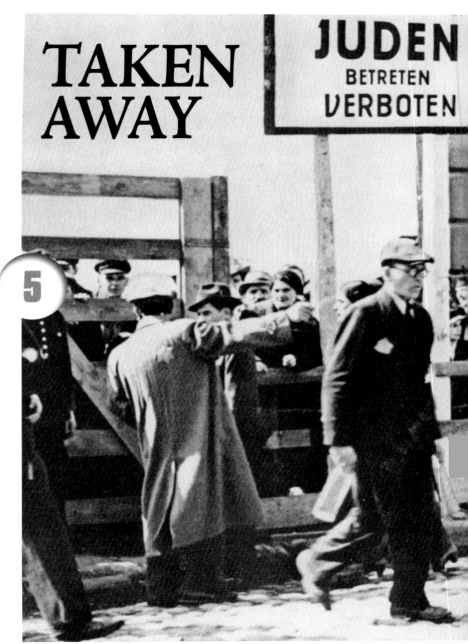

TAKEN AWAY

JUDEN
BETRETEN
VERBOTEN

Signs outside of the Lodz Ghetto stated that this was the Jewish District.

Dawid Sierakowiak

After the Sierakowiak family had made themselves a meager dinner of watered-down potato soup, they saw the cars and wagons pull into the ghetto. They could see that the vehicles carried a team of German-led officials, including medical examiners, nurses, police officers, and men from the fire brigade.

Dawid Sierakowiak watched through the window as some of the officials sealed off the house across the street. He sat for over an hour, watching and wondering what might be happening in there. Finally, the door burst open and police officers brought out three children. The children screamed and struggled against the authorities. Their mother's wails were like nothing Dawid had ever heard before.

Soon the street was filled with shrieks and wails as children were dragged away from their families. It seemed to Dawid that the poor parents were going insane.

"Why are they doing this to us?" Nadzia, Dawid's younger sister, cried. She pressed her head into her mother's shoulder.

Dawid looked around the room at his family. A nervous knot tightened in his stomach as he wondered what would become of them. His mother had become so thin, in part because she kept sharing her provisions with Nadzia and their father.

Before he had any more time to wonder, a group of officials entered their building and began examining the family. The doctor lingered around Dawid's mother, apparently searching for any sort of illness or disease.

"Very weak, very weak," the doctor said to the man beside him. Over and over again he used those two words to describe Dawid's mother. A great fear gripped him each time the doctor said these words.

"She seems quite fine," interjected a nurse who was assisting in the examination.

"No, she is very weak," the doctor repeated. "Send her away."

Dawid's throat tightened as he fought back the urge to cry. Nadzia's tears flowed freely as their mother hugged each of them.

"You have given your life by lending and giving away your provisions," Dawid said as his mother kissed his cheek.

She looked into his eyes, gave him a small smile, and nodded. "And I do not regret that," she said, before kissing his forehead one last time.

Then she was taken away.

Fred Spiegel
Gennep, Holland, September 20, 1942

Fred Spiegel and his cousin, Alfred, attended the Yom Kippur Eve service without Uncle Max, who had stayed home because he wasn't feeling well. The boys settled into a pew on the floor level with the other men, each in the traditional white Yom Kippur robes. The women, keeping with tradition, sat on the second floor. The service had just begun when a young man burst into the synagogue shouting.

"The Gestapo is coming to arrest all the Jewish men," he said breathlessly. "They're sending them to a concentration camp called Mauthausen."

The cantor, who had been performing the opening prayer for the service, fell silent. An eerie calm fell over the crowd as each man slowly removed his white robes. The cantor resumed his prayers as, one by one, each man left the synagogue.

Fred watched through the opened door as the men walked toward their homes. It seemed odd to him that no one ran or seemed to panic. The entire scene played out like a slow-motion dream. All the while the cantor continued to pray, until only Fred, Alfred, and a few other young boys remained. Even the women had gone.

The praying stopped and the cantor looked at the boys. "Would you please go home? I must leave now."

The boys walked out the open door with the cantor. Fred could see a few of the men still walking home in the distance.

Fred Spiegel

Fred was just a few days shy of his eleventh birthday when the Germans came for his family. In the early morning hours, Fred, his sister Edith, Uncle Max, Aunt Paula, and their children, Alfred and Ruth, had been picked up by a truck and taken to a railroad station in Nijmegen.

Many of the non-Jewish villagers stood by and watched as the family was loaded into a train car with so many other Jews. There was little anyone could do, even if any of them had wanted to help. Any interference would have resulted in death. And so they simply watched in silence as the Jews were taken away.

Later that day they arrived at a camp in Vught, Netherlands. Fred and his family were taken to the Jewish section of the camp, where they were immediately separated from one another. Children were not allowed to remain with their parents or relatives, and boys and girls were sent to separate barracks. Fred and Alfred remained together.

Fred watched his sister being taken away with the other girls. He prayed that she would be safe without him there to protect her.

"What have we done to deserve this?" Fred said quietly to Alfred. Alfred could only shake his head.

There was nothing any of them had done wrong, it was simply being Jewish that had set them apart.

The Nazis deported massive numbers of Jewish men, women, and children on European railways.

In the early dawn hours, Fred and Alfred walked from the barracks they had slept in toward the train. Their family had been at Vught for little more than a month before they were all transported together to Westerbork. And now it seemed they would be moved yet again, just one day after arriving. They each carried the small number of belongings they had been allowed to bring with them from Vught.

Fred felt frightened as he saw that many of the others walking toward the train were crying. He scanned the crowd for his separated family members, but did not see any of them.

"Do you see your parents? Or Edith?" Fred asked Alfred, his voice tight with anxiety.

Alfred looked up and down the platform filled with other detainees, some weeping, others walking numbly toward the railcars.

"No, I don't see anyone," he replied, a quiver of panic in his words. They had already been separated from Alfred's sister, Ruth, who had been detained at Vught.

As the boys drew close to the entry of the railcar, they saw it was already packed full of people. Fred felt large hands press against his back as the dry voice of a Nazi soldier ordered them to hurry up.

"No," Fred said. "No." His voice felt small and seemed to get lost in the noise of the crowd.

The soldier continued shoving Fred and Alfred into the train, pushing them into the tangle of bodies. But when Fred's foot crossed over the threshold, he began to scream as he had never screamed in his life. Soon, Alfred's screams echoed his own, and both boys protested with all their might.

"What's all the screaming about?" one SS guard asked a nearby Dutch police officer.

"The children are afraid and do not want to go on the train," the officer replied.

The SS guard immediately ordered the Jewish camp police officer to remove Fred and Alfred from the train. The boys were placed in a small room, where they were held until the train departed. Eventually, they were returned to their barracks, where they heard from Uncle Max that he had made arrangements to ensure that none of them would be transported on the trains leaving the camp. Fred took some comfort in his uncle's assurance, but deep inside he worried that nothing was certain anymore.

Fred Spiegel
Westerbork, Netherlands, July 2, 1943

Fred stood beside Alfred in the barracks. The sky outside hung onto the darkness of night, not quite ready to give up its power to the sun that would soon rise.

"He called my name," Alfred whispered.

Fred looked into his cousin's wide, fearful eyes and tried to reassure him. "I'm sure Edith and I will not be far behind you. We will find you at the next camp."

Alfred began crying. "I don't think so," he said quietly.

Alfred packed his few things and lined up with the others who had been called. Tears still streamed down his cheeks as he looked back once more before walking away with the group.

Dawid Sierakowiak

Lodz Ghetto, March 22, 1943

"We are down to our last potatoes," Nadzia said quietly as she prepared what she could for dinner with the few rations they had left.

"We will have to make them last a few more days," Dawid replied. "Perhaps I could pick up a student or two to tutor to get more money."

"But you have been so ill," Nadzia said. "I worry about your fever. It has been going on for so many days."

Dawid's skin had become irritated and he was covered in scabs. He had seen the doctor a couple weeks before and was told that the fever was due to the scabs on his skin. The doctor told him to apply compresses and rest as much as possible, but with the number of deportations occurring in the ghetto, he was afraid to rest too much. Dawid had to show that he could still work or he knew he would be selected to be sent away. Although the siblings rarely spoke about what it would mean to be selected, Dawid knew in his heart that it meant certain death.

"How is the frostbite on your toe?" Nadzia asked.

"It seems to be getting better," he lied. The frostbitten toe was no better today than it had been weeks before. It was painful to walk, but he tried to hide the agony.

"There is talk of more deportations. I heard that the Germans have rounded up more people today," Dawid said, wanting to change the subject from his own poor health.

Nadzia put a dish of soup in front of him. His bowl had twice as much soup as hers. She saw him looking from one bowl to the other, and before he could comment on their contents she said, "You need your strength to get well, especially with the increased selections."

"You need your strength as well…" Dawid began.

"Do not argue. Just eat. Then get to bed and rest. I cannot have you taken away and be left here without you."

Udel Sadowski

Udel Sadowski's family had once included nine siblings and his parents, but had slowly dwindled down to one sister and one brother. Remaining in his family unit Udel also had his own wife, along with their fourteen-month-old child, his brother's wife, and his mother-in-law.

It had been two months since the Nazis surrounded the ghetto outside of Bedzin on June 22, 1943. Everyone inside the ghetto had been afraid, including Udel and his family. When the SS soldiers rounded up thousands of Jewish youths and immediately transported them away, rumors began to circulate that they had been sent to the concentration camp, Auschwitz.

Up until this point, the selections made by the Germans had been based on the Jews' ability to work. If a Jewish person was strong and his or her job was useful and important to the function of the ghetto or the factories the Germans supplied with workers, that person was allowed to stay. But that day, the Germans demonstrated that they were not just ridding the ghetto of the weak, but also sending away the young, healthy, and vibrant youths who had much to offer in the way of labor.

And so an even greater fear settled over the ghetto, and Udel began to hear whispered stories of people creating hiding places in their apartment walls and underground. For his part, he had carefully constructed a hideout within the walls of the family's ghetto apartment. Udel built a false wall about 3 feet away from the original apartment wall, and then created a hidden doorway inside a cupboard.

When the Germans declared that no Jews would be allowed to remain in Bedzin and all would be transported to concentration camps, Udel and his remaining extended family crawled through the secret doorway. Inside the cramped space between the walls, they lay on the floor as quietly as possible for several days.

There were no windows, and air could only come

into the cramped, hot space through small holes in the bricks the family had chiseled away. On the seventh day, the thick, suffocating air of the space finally took its toll on those stowed away inside.

"Our baby hasn't moved for quite some time," Udel's wife said, the panic in her voice evident even through her whisper.

Udel sat up and reached across his wife to their baby. The child was no longer breathing. He picked up the baby and held the lifeless body tenderly in his arms.

"Our child is gone," he said solemnly.

His wife sobbed, her jagged breaths breaking the otherwise silent calm of the hiding place. She leaned into Udel, rested her head on their only child, and cried until she had no more tears to shed.

"There is nothing to keep us here anymore," she whimpered. "What do we have to protect if our child is already dead?"

The others in the space shared her heartache. The baby had been their final hope. They would have died to protect the child. Now their hope was lost, and they agreed to surrender themselves to the Gestapo.

Udel, along with his wife, brother, sister-in-law, and mother-in-law, walked calmly toward the Gestapo man who was positioned just outside their apartment where they had been hidden for a week.

"We would like to surrender ourselves," Udel said.

"Very well," the man replied politely.

"Should we bring our bundles?" Udel asked, motioning toward the small bags of personal items they had brought to the street with them.

"Yes, because you are young people, and you are being transported to work," the man said.

The family gathered their bundles and numbly headed toward an uncertain future.

Udel Sadowski

Auschwitz Concentration Camp, Poland, August 1943

As Udel and his family filed out of the railroad car, armed SS soldiers met them on the platform. A member of the Gestapo stood between the SS men and the freshly imported prisoners.

Several men began to pull bodies out of the train car, tossing them into trucks. Some of the people they threw into the trucks were dead. Others were still alive, but unable to stand up because they were exhausted or overheated. Many were children who had surely suffocated in the heat of the unventilated cars. Udel counted 34 suffocated people pulled from the car they had been in.

The Gestapo man paced in front of the prisoners. He pointed a short stick at each person before indicating to which side of the platform he or she should go. The Gestapo man stopped at Udel. "You, there," he said motioning toward the soldiers on the opposite side of the platform. Next was Udel's wife. "You, there." Again he pointed toward the soldiers. When he got to Udel's sister, he pointed toward the trucks. What little color she had in her face drained as she walked slowly toward the line of others who were too young, too old, or too weak to be useful. Soon Udel's sister-in-law and mother-in-law followed her.

No one said they would be killed, but everyone knew what was to become of the unfortunate people standing on that side of the platform. It was the end for them. They had put up a good fight, they had tried to survive, but in the end it came to this, and with the point of a stick by a man who didn't even know their name, their fate was sealed.

Udel fought tears as he watched the women stand beside each other weeping silently. Although his heart was breaking, it was not a time to show weakness. Not if he hoped to survive.

Udel's brother joined him on the side of those who would be allowed to live another day. Their line was marched to the west barracks of Auschwitz.

"Quick! Hurry," the ruler of the camp ordered. "Move it! Strip completely!"

With that Udel found himself fumbling to remove his clothes. There was no time to be embarrassed, he simply had to obey as quickly as he could to avoid being kicked or hit with sticks by the SS men.

Soon he found himself being shaved—more like an animal than a human—until his head and entire body were hair-free. People around him screamed out at the rough treatment by their barbers. The sound of SS men striking blows against anyone who didn't cooperate quickly enough echoed in Udel's ears.

They were rushed through a shower, and then given mismatched, ill-fitting clothing. After that, they were led to the barracks where they would sleep, two men to a bed. The beds, stacked three high, were rickety bits of wood tacked together. There were no mattresses, only tattered blankets.

Finally, each prisoner was tattooed with a number that would become his or her identity, stripping them of even their names. The Nazis did everything they could to make them into animals, but Udel clung to his humanity, even though he could only hide it beneath the tattered shreds of his clothing.

Prisoners in Nazi concentration camps were not given much to eat, and the food they were given was often very poor quality. This led many people to suffer from starvation.

Udel Sadowski

Each day living in the concentration camp was unbearable, yet somehow, Udel found a way to bear it. The prisoners worked eight-, ten-, or even twelve-hour days. One day they carried rocks or dug ditches, another day they made lawns or concrete walkways to "beautify" the camp.

Udel found the idea laughable. How could they make beautiful a place where humans were dying regularly from hunger and exhaustion? Their lifeless bodies were heaped into wagons and wheeled away by skeletal prisoners. They were taken to the crematorium, whose chimneys poured smoke into the sky day and night as the bodies burned. Nothing they did could bring beauty to such a horrid place.

Other prisoners, known as kapos, guarded the workers day and night. The kapos were often Jews themselves, but had been selected to receive special privileges if they would keep their fellow Jews in line. They were often more cruel than the SS men because they had to prove themselves to avoid punishment or death. Udel swore he'd die before he took such a post. He sometimes wondered what he might do to survive, but every time he saw one of his comrades fall under the blows of a kapo he felt certain he would never resort to that.

This day was even more unbearable than most. Each Saturday the prisoners were stripped and made to stand in line while a German doctor inspected their bodies for any signs of illness. If he saw any sort of skin eruption, he would order the prisoner to be sent to the gas chambers for execution. This day, Udel's brother had been selected.

Now they lay one last time in the bed they shared since the first day they had arrived.

"I hate that there is nothing I can do to stop this!" Udel said, weeping.

"I know if there is anything that could be done, you would do it," his brother said numbly.

"They have already taken my wife, and now you. I would trade myself for both of you if they would let me." Udel's body shook with his sobs. "I will be the only one of our family to remain."

"Then you must stay alive, for us. If you do not, there will be no one to remember us. It will be as if we never existed at all."

Udel hugged his brother tightly, and both men cried together. In the early morning, they took his last living family member away. The wails that rose into the predawn sky each Sunday rose to meet the gray clouds of smoke that hung over the camp like a dark blanket. This time, Udel's dear brother's cries were among them.

Inside a gas chamber at Auschwitz. An estimated 1 million to 2.5 million people were killed at the camp.

THEY COULD ONLY PRAY

6

The Nazis routinely separated Jewish children from their parents.

Maria Blitz

The Nazis surrounded the ghetto. All of the Jews within had been ordered to pack their bags and prepare for transfer. The ghetto was to be liquidated, and the residents would be moved to a new location.

Maria Blitz stood on the sidewalk with her family in front of their apartment. Her three-year-old niece stood beside her. The little girl leaned her head against her mother.

A group of SS soldiers came down the center of the street.

"Line up. It's time to go," one soldier commanded. "Leave your bundles where they are. They will be sent behind you."

Maria hesitated to walk away from her things, but under the circumstances she didn't have much choice but to obey.

The family began to line up. Then they were marched to a street where thousands of other ghetto residents were gathered.

"You will all be transported to work camps," a Gestapo man said, addressing the crowd. "Your personal items will be sent along after you."

A low rumble of whispered concern rippled through the crowd.

"All children will remain at the hospital until they can be sent to the children's camp," the man continued.

"I cannot leave without my child," Maria's sister-in-law said frantically, hugging her daughter tightly. The crowd's whispers turned to desperate cries.

"Send your children forward to line up," the Gestapo man said firmly. SS soldiers began pulling frightened children from the crowd. The air was flooded with sounds of weeping. A woman Maria recognized, Dr. Blau, stepped forward. Dr. Blau was a kindly resident of the ghetto known for her habit of helping anyone in need.

"I will stay with the children," she said calmly. Parents still hesitated to send their children forward, but one by one, youngsters began to line up around Dr. Blau. Soon, Maria's niece stood among them, and the lines of weeping adults were marched away, leaving their beloved little ones behind. They could only pray that God would keep them safe.

Maria Blitz

Krakau-Plaszow Concentration Camp, Poland, Spring 1944

"I need to hide," the 16-year-old boy said desperately as he ran into the brush factory where Maria was assigned to work. "Please don't tell them I am here."

Before she could respond the boy was gone, hidden among the machinery. Shortly afterward the door opened and SS soldiers entered the room.

"Where is the boy?" one of them demanded.

Maria continued on with her work as she replied, "I do not know."

One of the men stepped in front of her and glowered down at her. "We need to have a certain number of Jews to fill our quota. Either you tell us where the boy is, or we will take you in his place."

Maria was not afraid. She looked up at the man and calmly replied, "I do not know where any boy is."

At that moment, the kapo in charge of the plant stepped forward. "I saw him run through. I believe you'll find him over there," he said, pointing toward a corner of the room.

The soldiers walked across the room, plucked the boy from his hiding place and dragged him toward the door.

"I know they are going to kill me!" he cried. "I want to live! I am only 16 years old!"

The boy's screams echoed off the walls and rafters of the factory. His voice could be heard through the corridor and out into the yard, until it slowly faded into the distance.

Eva Heyman

"They will be moving all the Jews to ghettos," Mariska said, bursting into Eva Heyman's home.

Mariska had been the family's cook before laws were enforced that made it illegal for non-Jews to work for Jewish employers. Although she was no longer their employee, she had remained a loyal friend, and loved Eva as if she were her own child.

Eva's grandmother was ironing men's shirts on the porch when Mariska burst in. She continued to iron as if she had not heard the words at all.

"You are allowed to take along only one change of underwear, the clothes on your bodies, and the shoes on your feet," Mariska continued as she hastily began packing.

Eva was dazed by Mariska's words. She thought she must be in a nightmare, but she knew in her heart that this was no dream.

Maria Blitz

It had been a few weeks since the women had been forced to walk naked before the Germans in the center of the camp. The soldiers had selected those who appeared to be too old or too weak to be of much use and written down their names.

Maria Blitz's 56-year-old mother had been selected, and she had spent the last few weeks worrying about her fate.

"They're going to take me away and gas me," she had said.

"No, mother," Maria had said, trying to assure her. "You are too young. You have much usefulness left in you." But she had no faith in the words she spoke.

Now, they stood in the same spot, all the women lined up once again. This time they were permitted to remain clothed. Maria felt panic rising in her as the soldiers began to call out women's names. One by one, the men ran down the list they had made weeks before until they came to Maria's mother's name. The world seemed to stop in that moment as she watched her mother move forward. After the condemned were marched away, the rest of the prisoners were dismissed to their barracks.

"I have no mother anymore," Maria said, as she threw herself onto the floor and wept. "I have lost my mother."

Oliver Lustig

Cluj Ghetto, Romania, June 6, 1944

Oliver Lustig had been living with his family in the ghetto in Cluj for about a month. They had been sent there after every Jew in his home village of Soimeni, Hungary, had been arrested and deported.

Now he stood on the platform with his family, waiting to board another train to be transferred to another camp, along with thousands of other Jewish prisoners. At the age of 17, Oliver was the oldest son remaining with the family. His 21-year-old brother had already been taken to a forced-labor camp.

Oliver's 8-year-old brother, Valentin, stood beside him, along with his mother and his 14-year-old twin siblings, Cornel and Cornelia. His mother gave him an unsure smile. She tried to hide her fear to keep her children calm, but Oliver saw the uncertainty in her eyes.

An SS man ordered them to move into the train car in front of them. His father, 19-year-old sister, Eva, and 16-year-old brother, Emilian, boarded in front of him.

Oliver's mother hurried in behind him with the twins before the door slid shut. "Stay together," she called as the family became lost in the commotion of bodies inside the train car. Oliver grabbed Valentin's hand and edged his way through the tangle of bodies toward his father.

Eva Heyman

Eva Heyman had been living in the ghetto with her family for just over a month. They were only given a bowl of beans and 7 ounces of bread to eat each day. It was barely enough to keep them alive.

They had been assigned a room to share with 13 others, including Eva's immediate family and her cousin, Marica, whom she slept beside each night on the floor.

Often during her time in the ghetto, she had thought of her friend Marta Munzer and even dreamed about her at night. "She was just a girl," Eva confided in her diary, "And still the Germans killed her. But I don't want them to kill me! I want to be a newspaper photographer, and when I'm 24, I'll marry an Aryan Englishman…"

One day, her family discussed their possible fate. Many people believed the Germans would eventually kill them.

"I don't want to die," Eva said firmly.

"I am not afraid of dying," her grandmother responded.

Looking around the room at her family's faces, each trying to process the idea that they might not survive this nightmare, Eva declared, "But she is 72, and I'm only 13!"

Now, Eva filed toward the train in a group of 500 people. The words "German Worker Resettlement" were written on the train. She prayed those words were true. She would give anything to harvest a field or tend to pigs or sheep, anything to be allowed to live this life she had only just begun to live.

Oliver Lustig
Auschwitz Concentration Camp, Poland, June 9, 1944

They had been on the train for four days and three nights with no room to lie down. All the 80 people had to eat were the little bits of food stowed away in their luggage and, to drink, one bucket of water for the entire group. When one passenger died during the trip, the lack of space forced the other passengers to prop up the body with the luggage against the wall of the train.

"Everybody out!" an SS soldier shouted as the doors to the car squealed open.

The exhausted, dehydrated prisoners rushed to get out.

"Leave any luggage behind!"

Oliver Lustig followed the soldier's orders, but he hated to leave his luggage behind. Although it wasn't much, it was all he had left in the world. He stepped out of the car onto the ramp, leaving behind the last of his worldly possessions. At least he still had his family. He knew others were not so lucky.

"You have finally reached your destination," a Gestapo man said, almost cordially. "My apologies to you all for the conditions in which you were forced to travel here. We had no control over that. You have now arrived at a labor camp where you will get enough food, and you will have decent living conditions if you work well."

Oliver was surprised at the polite reception. The conditions in the ghetto had been so awful that he now felt relieved to be in a place where he could work and earn at least a small level of comfort with adequate food. Maybe if he worked really hard, he could earn extra rations for his younger brothers.

"Unfortunately, we have some bad news for you," the man continued. "There are still 3 kilometers to go till you reach the camp where you will live and work. And it just so happens that today we don't have enough vehicles to take you there. So will the mothers, the children under fourteen, the sick, and the invalids please get to the other side of the ramp? We will find the vehicles necessary to transport them somehow. The others will walk to the camp."

Oliver's mother gripped Valentin's hand and stepped to the other side of the ramp with Cornel and Cornelia. Oliver remained where he was, along with his father, Eva, and Emilian.

Of the thousands of people on the ramp that afternoon, more than half of them were now on the side with Oliver's mother and younger siblings. There was no time for a hug or kiss, but it didn't seem necessary since they would see one another soon enough in the camp.

Oliver watched his mother, still holding Valentin's hand, the twins close to her side, as they moved with the crowd away from the ramp. He watched until they disappeared from his sight.

A train car full of Jewish families arrives at Aushwitz.

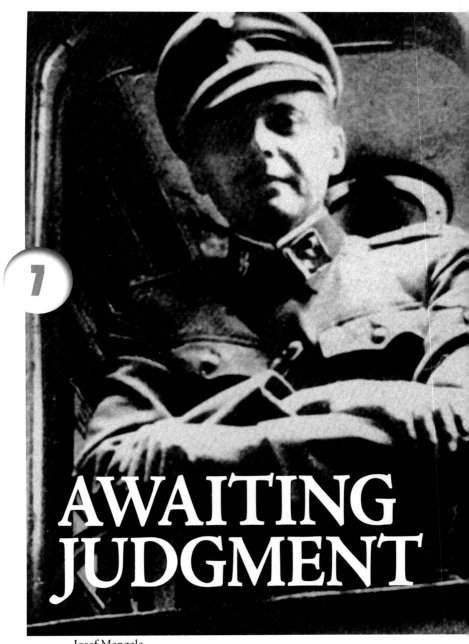

7

AWAITING JUDGMENT

Josef Mengele

For three hours Oliver stood naked and at attention in front of the barracks. He was one of many young men between the ages of 14 and 20 who awaited judgment from the SS captain, Doctor Josef Mengele. Mengele would decide who would live another day and who would not.

Lined up in rows of five, the boys did not dare speak or move. Oliver's body trembled, partly from exhaustion and partly because he was certain he would not pass this selection. He was by far the skinniest boy in his row. He was terrified not only for himself, but for every boy in his row. He had heard that if one boy was considered unfit to live, the entire row was sent to the gas chambers.

Oliver had tried to move to a different line— one with other boys who were smaller like he was. He did not want to be the one to sentence the boys who had become his friends to death. But his friends had grabbed him and kept him in their line.

The tallest and strongest boy of the group stood like a human shield in front of him. Oliver prayed Mengele would overlook his puniness for all of their sakes.

But now Mengele ordered that each boy walk alone in front of him. Oliver's heart seemed to stop at the news. Five SS soldiers stood near Mengele as the boys walked past for inspection. The soldiers watched the index finger on Mengele's right hand. If that finger twitched, the boy who was being inspected was sentenced to death. Each time this signal came, the five soldiers descended upon the unlucky boy like a pack of lions, hurling him to the end of the line.

Two brothers stood in line before Oliver. The older one, who was strong and well built, went first. He passed quickly, without incident. His younger brother walked behind him. He was not so lucky. When the soldiers grabbed the boy, the older brother turned around. Oliver wondered if he would attack the soldiers to try to help his brother.

But before he moved, the younger brother screamed, "No! Stay there! You must live! At least one out of the entire family must survive!"

Seeing this disruption, Mengele became enraged. "Kill him!" he yelled.

In the ruckus, Oliver walked in front of Mengele. His body became weak and he began to collapse, but the boys behind him quickly supported his weight and hurried him toward the barracks. The chaos proved to be enough of a distraction to allow him to pass by unnoticed. He survived another day, but he wondered how many more days he would have. He feared it would soon be his turn to make that long, final journey to death.

But even greater than his fear of death was his desire to live.

Oliver Lustig

Auschwitz Concentration Camp, Poland, Late Summer 1944

Oliver gazed toward what was known as the Roma Camp. From the day he had arrived at Auschwitz, he had known that the Roma prisoners were housed in the barracks just across an alley from his own. At least they had been until the swift and powerful hatred of the Nazis swallowed them up. Oliver had heard their screams a night ago. He'd heard the voices of women, children, and men, all wailing and cursing at the SS soldiers. They had not gone quietly.

But now all was quiet. Every last Roma prisoner was gone. Their barracks stood in utter silence, the doors left open by the people who had been torn away, never to return. In the distance the smokestack of the crematorium spurted flames, and thick curls of bluish-black smoke wafted through the sky, carrying more ashes back over the camp.

Eva Heyman

Auschwitz Concentration Camp, Poland, October 17, 1944

Eva Heyman had survived the deportation from the Nagyvarad Ghetto, packed with nearly 100 others in a stifling hot railroad car with only one pail of water for the trip. Others had not been so lucky. But she still saw her future in her mind. She dreamed of it and prayed that she would be allowed to live out the plans she had for herself.

For four and a half months, Eva endured the type of mental and physical agony that caused others to buckle and welcome death, but she continued to fight. Even after her cousin Marica passed away in her arms, Eva was determined to live. Her will was strengthened when she heard rumors that Allied troops were closing in on the camp.

Then came the frightening news that Doctor Mengele would make another round of selections. The prisoners were made to line up. As Mengele passed in front of the prisoners, he stopped near Eva. She tried to stay out of sight behind another woman.

"Come out from there so I can see you," *Mengele ordered.*

Eva complied, her legs nearly buckling beneath her from fear. Her feet were covered in sores and she wished she could hide them.

Mengele inspected her. When his eyes moved to her feet he said, "You frog. Your feet are foul, reeking with puss! Up with you on the truck!"

"No, please," Eva cried.

She wanted to resist, but she knew if she did not

cooperate they would simply shoot her. She walked toward the truck, but hesitated before climbing aboard. She was desperate not to die, but she felt powerless to fight the forces that decided her fate.

"In with you," Mengele said, before shoving her into the mass of doomed people on the truck.

Eva looked sadly toward the crematorium where she knew her dreams would be consumed by the flames—her hopes transformed into a cloud of smoke that would rain down on the camp where she had struggled so bravely to stay alive. Her fighting spirit would be gone, and only her ashes would remain.

Udel Sadowski

Auschwitz Concentration Camp, Poland, January 21, 1945

"Get up, all of you!" the SS soldier ordered.

It seemed to Udel Sadowski that he had just laid down. But that was not an unusual feeling. Often the prisoners got only four or five hours of sleep before being awoken for roll call, but this moment seemed somehow different. Udel had been chosen, along with

650 other Jewish prisoners at Auschwitz, to move to Camp Fünfeichen in Germany, where he would help build artillery.

"Stand in formation," another man commanded. "Move it!"

Soon all the inmates were lined up. Each prisoner was handed a blanket and about 2 pounds of bread. Then they were ordered to march. Although they had been told they were moving on to a new location to work, there had been whispers around the camp that the Allied troops were closing in. Udel prayed it was true.

Maria Blitz

Near Konigsberg, Prussia,
Late January 1945

The Jewish women had been marching for days through the snow and ice, wearing only wooden clogs on their feet. Their ragged clothing had been pieced together with paper, wires, and anything else they could find. Each had been given a thin blanket, so tattered the wind blew through the threadbare fabric.

Maria Blitz's sister, Gita, was struggling to continue marching. The sisters had walked the countless miles together. But now, the many days of the journey, and severe diarrhea, had taken their toll.

"I don't have the strength to go on," Gita said, as her footsteps began to slow.

"You can," Maria said. "You must."

Gita dropped to the ground, "I am too tired."

Maria and another woman tried to pull Gita to her feet, hoping the SS soldiers would not notice. "Get up! They will kill you," Maria pleaded.

"I can't," Gita replied. "I want to go to Mother."

Tears welled up in Maria's eyes. Their mother had died many months before in Auschwitz, and now her sister had resigned herself to die too.

"Please, Gita. Please, get up and try to keep going," she begged.

"Leave me lying here, please. I just want to go to Mother."

At that moment an SS man approached. Seeing Gita on the ground, he pulled out his gun and shot her without hesitation. Before Maria could react to seeing her last living sister killed right in front of her, one of the other prisoners grabbed her arms.

"You must keep going," the woman said, pulling Maria back into formation.

Maria felt something inside of her that willed her to live, despite the horror of the moment. She marched on as tears formed small icicles on her lashes.

When night fell, Maria resolved that her only hope was to escape. As they marched past a field, she slowly moved away from the formation. SS soldiers were all around the women, but somehow she managed to make her way to the field unnoticed. She found an outhouse and hid inside. After huddling there for some time, she opened the door. The women and guards were gone from sight. Her legs had no more strength to carry her on, so she dropped to the ground and crawled on her hands and knees until she came to a stable. She slipped inside, buried herself under the warm hay, and slept.

As the sun came up, Maria awoke to the sounds of horses neighing. A man stood above her.

"Who are you?" he asked.

Maria was too terrified to speak. She feared she had crawled right back into the enemy's hands.

"Don't be afraid," the man said kindly. "I am a communist, and I am going to help you."

EPILOGUE

As Allied forces moved across Europe in July 1944, they found one concentration camp after another. The Nazis tried to hide evidence of the mass murders they had committed and forced those prisoners who could still do so to march deeper into Germany. Many thousands died during these marches. By the time Allied troops found the camps, only a small number of prisoners who had been too weak to march remained.

The soldiers were shocked at the sight of people so thin they hardly looked human. Even more shocking were the piles of bodies, left behind when the SS had run out of time to burn them. At Auschwitz, Allied soldiers discovered buildings filled with personal items taken from prisoners when they arrived. These items included hundreds of thousands of men's suits and more than 800,000 items of women's clothing. Stacked in bags were 14,000 pounds of human hair that the Nazis had been using to stuff into furniture for padding.

On April 30, 1945, Russian troops were closing in on the bunker where Adolf Hitler and his loyal staff and friends were hiding. Before the Russians arrived, Hitler and his wife, Eva Braun, committed suicide. The next day, Joseph Goebbels and his wife, Magda, tucked their six children into bed. As the children slept, a doctor put poison pills into their mouths. Then Goebbels and his wife committed suicide.

After being released from Dachau Concentration Camp in 1938, Arnold Blum emigrated to the United States. He enlisted in the army, returning to Germany before the war ended to serve as a liaison between American soldiers and the Germans. While there, Blum learned about a former Nazi, Herr Schluemper, who had been bragging about beating up Jews during Kristallnacht. One evening, Blum visited Schluemper's home in the nearby town of Blumenthal to confront him. Schluemper confirmed he had been a Nazi, but denied any involvement in Kristallnacht. Blum declared that Schluemper was a liar before landing an uppercut against his chin. He left Schluemper in a heap on the floor. Blum accomplished something few Holocaust survivors would ever enjoy—a small piece of retribution against someone whose hands had mercilessly beaten innocent Jews.

After her liberation, Maria Blitz married and moved to America. Looking at her sons, she was reminded of the children, including her three-year-old niece, who had been kept in the Krakow Ghetto. If their parents had known the Nazis would shoot them all before the day ended, they would have fought to protect them. But then they too would have been killed that day.

Blitz was haunted by such memories and plagued with nightmares. Despite surviving, she felt a part of her was dead, murdered by the Nazis along with her family. She made it her goal to help others remember in the hope that such horrors would never be repeated.

In the summer of 1989, Fred Spiegel took his family on a trip to Europe so they could better understand the life he lived, and the childhood he lost. They visited his father's and grandmother's graves and stopped by the memorial at Bergen-Belsen to pay respects to the Jews buried in the mass graves there. Like ripping a bandage off an old wound, the trip was painful but necessary.

On the 55th anniversary of Kristallnacht, Spiegel returned to Dinslaken, Germany, to participate in a ceremony, along with other survivors of the Jewish community, to unveil a memorial dedicated to the victims. By then, he was speaking at schools about being a Holocaust survivor and the importance of forgiving but never forgetting.

Oliver Lustig served in the army for 37 years, working as a military journalist. He also earned a PhD in Economics. Lustig dedicated his life to helping others understand the truth of what happened during the Holocaust. He wrote several books of his own and translated Eva Heyman's diary from Hungarian to Romanian as a labor of love to the memory of all Holocaust victims.

All records of Herschel Grynszpan stopped in May of 1945. He was declared dead in 1960 with his date of death noted as May 8, 1945.

For three and a half years, Dawid Sierakowiak fought to stay alive under unimaginably difficult conditions, but on August 9, 1943, his death certificate was signed. The cause of his death was tuberculosis, starvation, and exhaustion, or what became known as "ghetto disease."

The lives of Sierakowiak and Eva Heyman were destroyed by the Nazis—along with an estimated 11 million other innocent victims, 6 million of them Jews—but the stories of their struggles to survive live on in both of their diaries. They represent the plight of the estimated 1.5 million children who were murdered by the Nazis. They could never have known the impact their words would have on people all over the world. Their voices cry out from beyond the grave, "Remember us! We lived!"

"Those who cannot remember the past are condemned to repeat it." — George Santayana

On January 27, 1945, Soviet troops entered Auschwitz, freeing more than 7,000 prisoners.

TIMELINE

July 29, 1921: Hitler becomes the Führer (leader) of the National Socialist German Workers' (Nazi) party.

April 20, 1923: The Nazi newspaper *Der Stürmer* begins publication of propaganda against Jews.

January 30, 1933: German president Paul von Hindenburg names Hitler chancellor of Germany.

April 1, 1933: Hitler declares a national boycott on Jewish businesses.

April 7, 1933: German Jews are banned from the civil services.

May 10, 1933: A nationwide book burning of all books written by Jewish authors occurs throughout Germany.

August 2, 1934: German president Paul von Hindenburg dies; the office of president is abolished and its powers are combined with those of the chancellor, giving Hitler complete control of Germany.

September 15, 1935: Nuremberg Laws are instituted revoking German citizenship to Jews and prohibiting the marriage of Jews to non-Jewish Germans.

November 14, 1935: Nuremberg Laws extend to others the Germans feel are racially inferior, including Roma (Gypsies) and blacks.

November 7, 1938: Herschel Grynszpan shoots Ernst vom Rath at the German Embassy in Paris, France.

November 9, 1938: Ernst vom Rath dies from the gunshot wounds inflicted by Hershcel Grynszpan; Joseph Goebbels incites the destruction of Jewish property that became known as Kristallnacht.

February 8, 1940: The Nazis officially announce that there will be a ghetto established in Lodz to house the estimated 230,000 Jewish population there.

May 1942: Herschel Grynszpan is transferred from Sachsenhausen Concentration Camp, and there is no further record of him after this point.

SEPTEMBER 4, 1942: Chaim Rumkowski, the Jewish head of the Council of Elders in the Lodz Ghetto, announces that the Nazis have ordered the transfer of about 25,000 ghetto inhabitants, mostly children and elders.

JUNE 22, 1943: Germans surround the ghetto outside of Bedzin, Poland, and announce that they will transport all Jews to Auschwitz Concentration Camp.

MARCH 13, 1944: The liquidation of the Krakow Ghetto begins.

APRIL 30, 1945: Adolph Hitler and Eva Braun commit suicide.

MAY 8, 1945: Nazi Germany's unconditional surrender is accepted by the Allies, ending the war in Europe.

SEPTEMBER 2, 1945: Japan formally surrenders to the Allies; World War II officially ends.

GLOSSARY

ambassador (am-BA-suh-duhr)—a person who represents their government in a foreign country

Aryan (AIR-ee-uhn)—a term used by Nazis to describe a supposed master race of pure-blooded Germans with blonde hair and blue eyes

barracks (BAR-uhks)—a large plain building or group of buildings where many people live

concentration camp (kahn-suhn-TRAY-shuhn KAMP)—a camp where people such as prisoners of war, political prisoners, or refugees are held

embassy (EM-buh-see)—a building in one country where the representatives of another country work

Gestapo (guh-STAH-poh)—the secret police of Nazi Germany

liquidate (LIK-wid-ayt)—the process by which the Nazis emptied the Jewish ghettos and sent all of the residents to concentration camps

Nazi (NOT-see)—a member of a political party led by Adolf Hitler; the Nazis ruled Germany from 1933 to 1945

propaganda (praw-puh-GAN-duh)—information spread to try to influence the thinking of people; often not completely true or fair

segregation (seg-ruh-GAY-shuhn)—practice of separating people of different races, income classes, or ethnic groups

synagogue (SIHN-uh-gog)—a Jewish place of worship

Yom Kippur (YOM KE-poor)—the holiest day of the year in the Jewish religion; Jewish people fast and ask for forgiveness during this holiday

CRITICAL THINKING USING THE COMMON CORE

1. Herschel Grynszpan wanted to make a statement to the world about the horrible conditions the Jews were being forced into. Do you think his actions made the situation better or worse for the Jews? Use evidence from the text to support your answer. (Key Ideas and Details)

2. Consider the discrimination the Jews faced even before World War II broke out. Compare this to the racial discrimination and segregation experienced by African Americans in the United States during the 1950s and 1960s. (Craft and Structure)

3. Some Jewish prisoners served as kapos for the concentration camps, supervising and disciplining other inmates to maintain order for the Nazis. Udel Sadowski said he would never accept a position as a kapo no matter what. Why do you think some Jews would accept the role of kapo? Do you think the decision to become a kapo could be justified? Use examples from the text to support your answer. (Key Ideas and Details)

INTERNET SITES

FactHound offers a safe, fun way to find Internet sites related to this book. All of the sites on FactHound have been researched by our staff.

Here's all you do:
Visit *www.facthound.com*
Type in this code: 9781491484548

FactHound will fetch the best sites for you!

FURTHER READING

Gratz, Alan. *Prisoner B-3087*. New York: Scholastic Press, 2013.

Langley, Andrew. *Hitler and Kristallnacht*. Chicago: Heinemann Library, 2014.

Leyson, Leon. *The Boy on the Wooden Box: How the Impossible Became Possible... on Schindler's List*. New York: Atheneum Books for Young Readers, 2013.

Lowry, Lois. *Number the Stars*. New York: Houghton Mifflin Harcourt, 2014.

Roy, Jennifer. *Jars of Hope: How One Woman Helped Save 2,500 Children During the Holocaust*. North Mankato, Minn.: Capstone Press, 2016.

Tarshis, Lauren. *I Survived the Nazi Invasion, 1944*. New York: Scholastic, 2014.

SELECTED BIBLIOGRAPHY

Adelson, Alan, ed. *The Diary of Dawid Sierakowiak: Five Notebooks from the Lodz Ghetto.* New York: Oxford University Press, 1996.

Berenbaum, Michael. *The History of the Holocaust as Told in the United States Holocaust Memorial Museum.* Boston: Little, Brown, 1993.

Boas, Jacob, ed. *We Are Witnesses: Five Diaries of Teenagers Who Died in the Holocaust.* New York: Macmillon, 2009.

Brostoff, Anita, ed. *Flares of Memory: Childhood Stories Written by Holocaust Survivors.* Pittsburgh: Holocaust Center of the United Jewish Federation of Pittsburgh, 1998.

Manvell, Roger, and Heinrich Fraenkel. *Doctor Goebbels: His Life and Death.* New York: Skyhorse Pub., 2010.

Marino, Andy. *Herschel: The Boy Who Started World War II.* Boston: Faber and Faber, 1997.

Niewyk, Donald L., ed. *Fresh Wounds: Early Narratives of Holocaust Survival.* Chapel Hill, N.C.: University of North Carolina Press, 1998.

Spiegel, Fred. *Once the Acacias Bloomed: Memories of a Childhood Lost.* Margate, N.J.: ComteQ, 2011.

INDEX

ABOUT THE AUTHOR

Jessica Freeburg lives in Lakeville, Minnesota, with her husband and three children. Her poetry and short stories have appeared in various magazines and anthologies. Her debut young adult novel, *Living in Shadows*, was released in 2015. She enjoys allowing her fascination with history to inspire her creatively, whether she's writing fiction or nonfiction, working on documentary films, or traveling to historic locations to experience the past firsthand. You can visit her online at www.jessicafreeburg.com or follow her on Twitter: @jessicafreeburg.